SMART HOME DESIGN

Ideas, Tips & Guide For Home Remodeling

By Laura Cerwinske

Featuring Airoom Architects & Builders, The Nation's Design & Build Leader

Dedicated to the loving
memory of Burton Klein,
who founded Airoom in 1958.
Without his pioneering vision,
this book would not be possible.

Ideas, Tips & Guide For Home Remodeling

SMART HOME DESIGN

By Laura Cerwinske

Photos Courtesy of Airoom, Inc. and Airoom Architects Inc.

Reed
PRESS™

We would like to acknowledge some of the fine manufacturers whose products appear in the photos of this book.

James Hardie Siding Products

Crystal Cabinet Works

Neff Kitchens

Majestic Fireplaces

Burton Allen Cabinetry

Ahnzu Stone

Andersen Windows

daltile

Therma-Tru

Franke

Thermador

Rohl Faucets

Schlage

Lennox

Juno Lighting

Owens Corning

First published in USA 2004 by Reed Press
Copyright© 2004 Reed Press

Art Direction & Graphic Design
  Judith K. Hall

Production Manager
  Paul Ojeda

Managing Editor
  Amanda Westbrooks

Publishing Director
  Kelly Keane

Author
  Laura Cerwinske
  Smart Home Design

p. cm.
ISBN 1-59429-033-4
1. Interior Design. American-Remodeling
2. Home. Improvement.

ISBN 1-59429-033-4
Printed in Hong Kong by Toppan Printing

Library of Congress Control Number:
2003098962

All photos courtesy of

AIROOM
ARCHITECTS & BUILDERS
— SINCE 1958 —

EVERYTHING TO IMAGINATION. NOTHING TO CHANCE.™

FOREWORD

Over the last twenty-five years, home design has captivated America. Increased travel has expanded our horizons and a new generation of so-called shelter magazines has fueled an interest in design at home. The average American house increased dramatically in size over this period, creating decorating opportunities as well as a pragmatic need for more furniture and furnishings. Encouraged by enlightened retailers, the public has developed an appetite for good-looking, well-made household objects at affordable prices. Homeowners today, accustomed to the value found in the retail marketplace, also expect such value in the design and construction of their houses.

The hectic pace of our lives has put increased emphasis on the functionality of rooms. Organization is more essential than ever. Creating a comfortable sense of domesticity still has the greatest importance but there is a growing realization that domestic character need not be elaborate to be successful.

These multiple facets of residential design today have left homeowners with questions and a yen for resources. How can ambitious homeowners make sense of all of this? Educate themselves! *Smart Home Design, Ideas, Tips and Guide For Home Remodeling* is one book to add to the list of valuable resources.

Michael Graves, FAIA
Michael Graves & Associates
Princeton, New Jersey
January 2004

TABLE OF CONTENTS

PHOTOS COURTESY OF AIROOM ARCHITECTS & BUILDERS

CHAPTER GUIDE

What *Are* The SMART Decisions?

The annals of home building and remodeling are filled with stories of dream houses and construction nightmares. For the process of home building and remodeling is both an art and a profession, requiring vision, planning, coordination, and great expertise. The smart homeowner seeks not only bright ideas and capable professionals, but, equally important, a succinct and effective means of coordinating art, trade, and the complicated finance of construction.

As a design writer and the author of more than fifteen books on architecture and design, I am always keen to identify sources of style and authority. When I learned of Airoom Architects and Builders, the nation's design/build leader in residential remodeling, I immediately recognized the unique value of their program and experience.

After nearly fifty years in business and with over 10,000 projects to their history, the firm has refined the complicated remodeling process to as near a science as an art form can be. Its 150-person staff coordinates as many as 300 projects at one time. Under the leadership of CEO, Mike Klein, their fluency enables homeowners to achieve what together they conceive, at a guaranteed price.

I was intrigued as much by their record of success as by their method, design, ingenuity and versatility.

Space is a valuable asset. Part of the equation is being practical and knowing how to get the most from working with professionals. By using Airoom as the "case study" for this book, the bar has been set to help manage, and further define, the expectation you should have when searching for a remodeling company. Writers, as professional communicators, appreciate the skill required to make abstract ideas and desires concrete. Airoom has finessed that process, beginning with articulation. Its staff probes: What is the scope of work? Can that scope be reasonably accomplished by the prospective budget and in the intended time? How great a consideration is resale value? Are the design ideas appropriate to region, climate, and neighborhood? Will all the elements of the project cohere?

In preparing this book, I have illustrated my fund of knowledge with examples of Airoom's expertise. The gallery of ideas is informed with both conceptual guidance and specific advice. It offers perspectives, approaches, cautions, and practical suggestions that clarify issues of design, construction, and technology. It uses Airoom's great archive of ideas and past projects to exemplify the many avenues of creative possibility.

The most valuable asset in residential remodeling is an educated client. Too many homeowners, even with expert design guidance, have watched despairingly as their ideal of perfect rooms collapses into a scenario of budgets, deadlines, and installations run amok. Even the simple remodeling of a kitchen involves as many as ten different trades. What's more, the design and deployment of electronic wiring has become as critical a factor in home design today as any mechanical, plumbing, or lighting system. As users of the Internet, of personal computers, and of sophisticated home entertainment systems, homeowners rightfully expect eloquent design and technical capability. This book offers the instruction that can make the difference between success and unrealized expectation.

Before

The architect, designer, or design team sketches a design that establishes the preliminary idea.

THE REMODELING PROCESS

The sketches are modified, usually with overlays, until the series resolves with a final sketch that articulates the fundamental elements and indicates details.

Before signing a contract, make sure that you understand all elements of your remodeling company's process. Most importantly, choose a company with which you feel comfortable. It is best to have an appointed contact person to manage communication between you and the company for the duration of your project. The design team should be aware of your personality and preferences — both should play a significant role in making your remodel unique.

The first realization is that once the basic wants and needs are defined, the creative process begins. Many spaces in the home have changed dramatically in the past few decades. Technical advancements happen quickly and constantly. It's a worthwhile endeavor to spend time browsing major showrooms, and search for a remodeling company with unique ability and long-standing reputation. Preferably, all of this can exist within one company, as is the case with Airoom.

FRONT ELEVATION

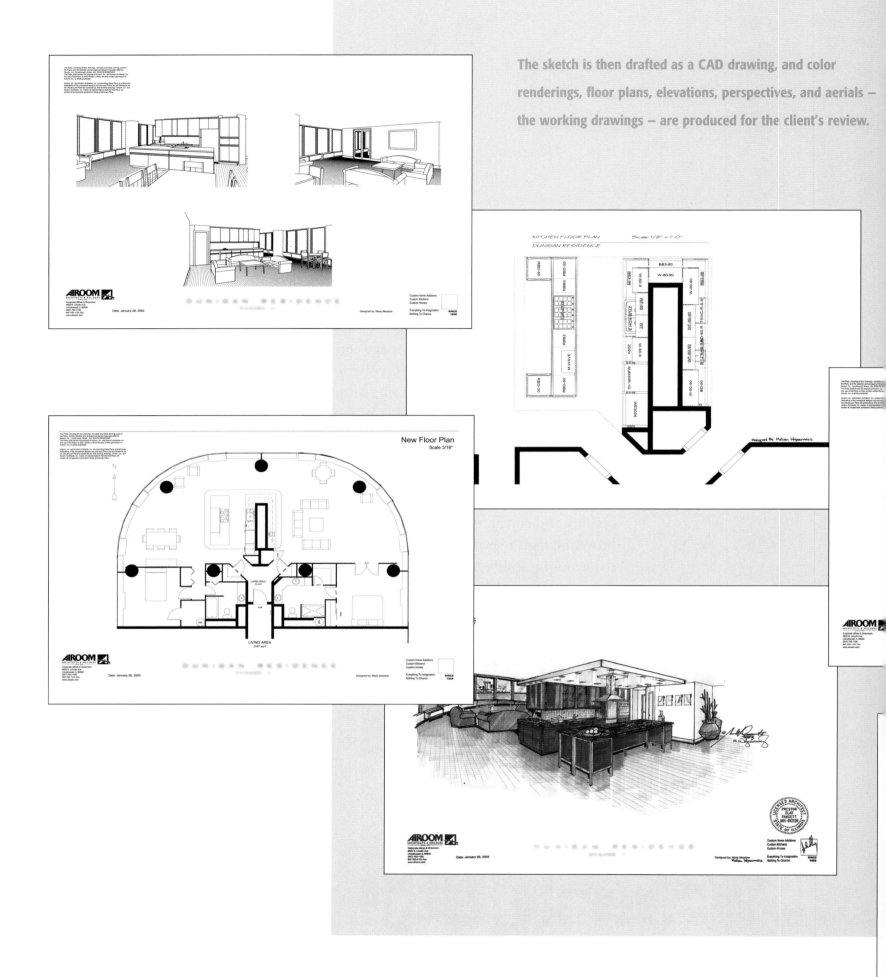

The sketch is then drafted as a CAD drawing, and color renderings, floor plans, elevations, perspectives, and aerials — the working drawings — are produced for the client's review.

Once the client approves this iteration, work moves from the office to the field: obtaining permits and zoning approvals, ordering materials, obtaining confirmations, purchasing materials, issuing work orders, beginning construction.

In your quest for a remodeling company, seek a business that employs an entire staff of architects and interior designers as well as building professionals. They will possess professional knowledge of what can and can't be done according to municipal building codes. In my experience, choosing a company that handles everything from design and permits — to construction and service — usually results in minimal stress for the client. In the end, a full-service organization will most likely save you money as well — especially if you value your personal time. A full-service organization will manage the design process, permits, and zoning issues, as well as supervise construction — so you can keep your day job!

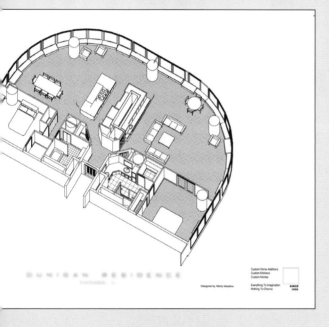

If you are working within a strict budget and cannot find a company that will aid with the financing of your remodel, the company you select should be aware of your restrictions. It is wise to anticipate that unexpected costs may arise so that you may plan a contingency fund.

Companies like Airoom, who have financing options in place, will make you aware of all costs up front — this type of remodeling company may better serve your desired level of comfort.

Ultimately, I have found that the success of any remodel can be expressed by Airoom's motto: *Design what you build, build what you design, and do it all at a fixed price.*

Trim, brick mold, and brick details are some of the least expensive means of adding depth and dimension to a façade. The more profiled the moldings and details, the more dramatic their effect.

Dramatic Transformation

Some homes undergo dramatic transformation. Before a client commits to the final design, they must feel comfortable with what a remodeling company has put forth.

In reading through the approach Airoom takes with its clientele, take note of some of the steps in the process that will establish your own personal comfort before embarking on the construction phase. Although not all remodeling companies will possess the same system, you can get a better idea of what to expect.

BEFORE

A dramatic transformation is the result of this whole-house remodel showing both the front and back views. The possibilities often exceed homeowner expectations.

BEFORE

BEFORE

EXTERIORS

Whether building a new kitchen, enlarging poorly proportioned rooms, constructing a sizable addition, or changing the style of a façade, every remodel requires solutions unique to the project and to its multitude of aspects. Even before the development of design, such issues as siting and terrain, zoning and permitting, climate factors, construction type, and neighborhood scale must be addressed.

According to Mike Klein, one of the most common mistakes in home design and remodeling is planning from the outside in. Focusing principally on the exterior design can lock a homeowner out of a good interior plan. It is far preferable to base that design on the interior floor plan so that issues such as light, and flow, and furniture layout are satisfactorily addressed. The smart homeowner will first consider the quantity and angle of natural light entering the rooms and will determine where exterior doors best serve interior circulation.

"Plan the exterior from the inside out. Rather than looking strictly at the footprint, design the dimensions around the interior. When fine-tuning the exterior, consider how a home may look at night and how the outdoor space may be used after sundown."

- Mike Klein, Airoom CEO

This was previously a ranch house that was converted into a two-story home with French influences.

The style of any home is largely communicated through the details. An architect must make sure that the proportion and scale of the detail matches the size of the home.

Style Considerations

Questions of style begin with formality: Is this house to be a formal residence or informal homestead? A symmetrical façade design typically implies formality; asymmetrical exteriors allude to the modern or more casual. Also, is the exterior design meant to replicate an historical style or to be an eclectic interpretation? And how will this style fit into the context of the neighborhood?

Similar questions must be asked of scale and integration. Again, how does the house fit scale-wise into the neighborhood? Is the remodeling or addition appropriate in proportion to the rest of the house or, for example, will the second floor be too tall for first floor? Are the rooflines smoothly integrated or will the exterior look like an amalgam of different pitches? Do the eaves of the overhangs correctly match the eaves of existing house? If not, is this dissimilarity deliberate?

Actually, dissimilar materials can work together in carefully crafted contexts. For example, decorative accents will break up the monotony of a surface or line as long as the detail material works with style of the house.

No exterior is complete in design without consideration of the landscape. Where will patios, terraces, pool or pond, cabana, and/or retaining walls be sited? Will the footprint of the house be articulated with hedges? What is the height and proximity of surrounding trees? Will accents, such as planter boxes, be built into the walls? How will the color palette of the garden and its plantings relate to the color scheme of the façade? What kind of lighting will best serve each?

Once inspired with an exterior design, it is also important not to be swept away by ideas that are not applicable to your needs. "Determine what you must have and what works. Leave the rest of the bells and whistles for another project," says Airoom's Chief Architect.

Landscaping puts a home in its proper context. Styles can range from bold wildflowers to meticulously groomed lawns and topiary. Consider landscaping to be the frame that's added to a favorite painting.

"Invite the outdoors indoors with a wall of folding glass doors."

- Mike Klein, Airoom CEO

Exterior Details

Often without great expense, the application of detail will make the difference between an ordinary design and a compelling one, between an undistinguished-looking façade and one with true distinction. Strength of statement, even in well-proportioned forms, typically derives from articulation. How, for example, does a wall meet the roofline? How deeply are the windows set back? What accents can be used, either subtly or conspicuously, to interrupt the visual monotony of a tall or long wall? In some cases, relocating a window by as little as twelve-inches, or the purchase of a $75 item can make the difference between a refined exterior and a clumsy one.

One of the best means of considering exterior details is to go to a manufacturer's web site, or make an appointment to visit a distributor or an architectural design/build showroom to view the actual application of details. Examine how details have been used and visualize them in the context of your own house. Remember that in residential design, more is not necessarily better. The value of a house is not measured by the pound. Detail typically looks best when concentrated in smaller areas rather than on a grand scale.

Garages

Rear entry, detached, and side garages preserve a formal or family-friendly exterior. When front garages must be used, creative plotting of houses on the lots and the use of varied setbacks along a street will improve the look of the neighborhood.

As long as zoning, structural, and foundation issues permit, it is always preferable to site the garage to the rear or side of the house, thereby preserving the elegance or friendliness of the facade. When a front garage is the only alternative, be careful that it is designed so that its volume or utility does not overpower the quality of the architecture. The style and size of the garage doors will be the principal factors in achieving this integration. The proper use of surrounding detail, such as patterned brick or siding, can further enhance it.

PHOTOS COURTESY OF AIROOM ARCHITECTS & BUILDERS

"Regardless of the style, size, or number of amenities that characterize a home, its ultimate success rests on its integration of form and function."
- Mike Klein, Airoom CEO

INTERIORS

The interiors of today's homes are cleaner and less adorned than a decade ago. This trend toward simpler details and more adherence to authentic architectural styles illustrates a move toward truer design cohesiveness. Fine craft and conceptual refinement are today's bywords.

Whether planning a space with little or no definition in an open-plan design, or working within parameters of a more compartmentalized floor plan, timelessness is a critical element. Turn to your own taste and preference to draw inspiration. Vintage pieces, or graceful, sleek, modern silhouettes can set the tone. If you have a taste for both, seek the input of the professionals you've contracted. A blend you never imagined may emerge.

Stairways

Stairs remain a focal point. Many staircases today are being installed on a sidewall, rather than in the center of the foyer. This creates added space to make the foyer more functional, with greater storage and display options for art and collectables. When stairs are located in the middle of the home, there is often a large area at the top that can be enhanced with large windows, bays, or a window seat.

Bring additional light into a home by adding windows that frame the front door.

Creative Use of Space

Nooks, small offices, and drop-and-go spaces are growing essential in today's kinetic family life. Many are located off the kitchen, and, depending upon size, function, and floor plan, offer space-efficient means of organization. In larger spaces, interior windows are often built into these nooks to allow in natural light.

A basement can host a variety of interesting possibilities such as a children's play area, wine cellar, exercise room, spa or sauna, or even an indoor pool. A small bedroom may be converted into a dressing room off the master suite. A long, narrow room may be transformed into a second laundry room.

Regardless of the style, size, or number of amenities that characterize a home, its ultimate success rests on its integration of practicality and pleasure.

Tastes change. Trends come and go. Self knowledge is the ultimate tool in creating a fulfilling interior.

Sometimes these transformations will stun the eye, sometimes simply delight it. The work of designing beautiful rooms is the art of orchestrating the timeless activities of domestic life.

PHOTOS COURTESY OF AIROOM ARCHITECTS & BUILDERS

A interesting conversion of a long narrow space off the mudroom or pool entrance is a second laundry room.

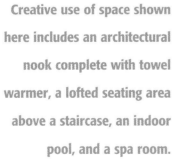

Creative use of space shown here includes an architectural nook complete with towel warmer, a lofted seating area above a staircase, an indoor pool, and a spa room.

PHOTOS COURTESY OF AIROOM ARCHITECTS & BUILDERS

Maximize storage and create a focal point
with a series of French doors.

COMMON SPACES

Regardless of the size of the house or the family, every home needs places for social gathering. Living rooms, great rooms, and family rooms accommodate parties, holiday events, and friendly entertaining. A formal living room is an excellent opportunity for lavish decorating, providing an ideal place to display art or showcase fine furniture. Great rooms and family rooms, typically more casual, are designed for relaxation and everyday use. "Regardless of their style, these rooms, as the most public of the house, must provide inviting areas for entertaining," says Mike Klein, Airoom CEO.

Furniture arrangement and lighting design should be determined according to the room's primary purpose or focus:
— Will entertaining center around the fireplace, television screen, or a card table?
— Will activities best be served by clusters of conversational seating arrangements or by a large, comfortable sofa/s and occasional chairs?
— What service furniture will the type of food and drinks served in this room require?
— Is wall display an important feature, and, if so, how will it be accommodated?

Floors

Flooring selection affects decisions about every other element of the room. The application of wood, stone, brick, tile, carpeting, or fine area rugs will define the character of the room just as color, material, texture, and design of the flooring will further enrich and refine the interior. In a formal living room, for example, a subtle backdrop will accentuate furnishings. In a casual, playful family room a boldly patterned floor will add visual energy. In a great room, where much activity takes place, carpeting may best subdue the level of sound.

Even - or especially — when great care is taken to select a flooring material, equal care must be given to the quality of installation. First, it is critical to address the condition of the existing floor. A sound, level sub floor and/or appropriate underlayment are essential. Even the best materials purchased at great cost can be rendered shoddy — looking if a floor is installed with inexpert hands or over a sub floor in poor condition.

Continuous flooring is typically preferable to the use of a variety of different materials that start and stop. The homogenous look created visually expands the space.

PHOTOS COURTESY OF AIROOM ARCHITECTS & BUILDERS

The airier and more volumetric a space, the better people feel in it.

Ceilings

Ceiling design is critical to a room's atmosphere because it greatly affects the room's proportions. "Ceiling height should be preserved or increased whenever possible," says Klein.

Living rooms, great rooms, and family rooms of sufficient proportions can be significantly enhanced with shaped ceilings such as trays, vaults, and domes that enlarge spatial volume.

The decorative treatment of the ceiling architecture also affects the feeling of volume. Vaults can be left exposed or finished with drywall or plaster and ornamented. Coffers — colored or decorated recesses in ceilings or partitions — look best in rooms with ceilings of at least 8' 6" in height and over. Beamed ceilings (open or encased) and cathedral ceilings originated purely for function. Now, they are often used simply for decorative effect. They typically impart a rustic look when trusses are exposed or stained. For sleeker, more contemporary looking interiors, flat ceilings often suffice. High, flat examples of 9 1/2 to 10 feet in height will give a public room a more formal, even museum-like feel. Crown moldings can also be applied for added effect.

Dropped ceilings and soffits can be used to lower the scale of a room in specific areas, such as over a table or sofa. A round shape may be used to mimic a circular dining table and further define the space. Soffits can also serve the practical purpose of hiding mechanicals while enhancing a room's architecture.

The ideal lighting design provides sufficient
illumination for a room's activities without
generating glare or excessive contrast.

Lighting

Different parts of a room require different types of lighting. A living room, family room, or great room is best served by a combination of lighting sources and treatments. Direct lighting, for example, illuminates a limited area, such as a game table or reading chair, where crisp, distinct vision is necessary. Indirect lighting reflects light off a ceiling or wall to produce a diffuse quality more suited to conversation or entertainment viewing areas. Concealed lighting emanates from coves or cornices to wash walls or other surfaces with soft lighting effects. Low voltage lamps are used to light artwork and provide accents.

The manner of installation further affects the room's style of illumination. A fixture hanging from the center of a ceiling tray will give the room a more traditional look. Perimeter or concealed lighting is more contemporary.

Soffits can be applied with as much versatility as the lighting they hold, offering, for example, a place for crown moldings to be installed. Cosmetic soffits are especially practical on vaulted areas because they allow lighting to fall squarely down to the floor and walls rather than at an angle. They can also be used to up light a perimeter, a treatment advisable only when the ceiling is of sufficient architectural or decorative merit. Curved soffits with built-in lighting create curved coves, which are exceptionally sculptural. "The use of effective lighting and its spectrum can turn the ordinary into the extraordinary," Klein says.

Nothing flatters a room like natural daylight.

Windows

Windows provide for light, ventilation, and views. These qualities are especially vital in a room as social as a living, family, or great room. Since domestic architecture affords a greater use of glass today than ever before - in both quantity and square footage - it is not surprising that rooms tend to feel 20 - 30% larger. Furthermore, with the added height of contemporary windows and window transoms, ceilings tend to feel higher.

Skylights, which are set directly into a flat or sloping roof, illuminate a room from above. Their variety of shapes affords great design flexibility. New technology of coatings and gasses allows for control of heat loss., heat gain and fading without obstructing light. These modern treatments should be used whenever possible.

Window frames — or casings — define the shape of the opening and should echo the style of the house. The window and its frame should also be designed in proportion to the scale and style of the room.

Accordingly, they may require or benefit from decorative treatment or embellishment.

H O M E   T H E A T E R S

Ideally, a home theater is designed in collaboration between the architect or designer and an audio/visual professional prior to construction, thereby determining optimal positioning and facilitating necessary wiring. The home theater is best configured as a rectangular room because of the audio and visual need for depth. Sonically "flat" floor coverings, such as carpeting or wood are preferable to tile, stone, or any surface that "bounces" sound. Similarly, wood doors are preferable to glass, and curtains better absorb sound than bare or paneled walls.

There are three types of theater screens: 1) The standard television type, or CRT (which stands for cathode ray tubes), is being phased out because of its bulk. While it provides a crisp, clear picture, it is heavy, deep and does not come any larger than 36-in. in size. 2) Plasma screens and LCDs (liquid crystal display) can be mounted anywhere (including table bases and tilt brackets) and viewed from any angle. Typically 40-in. and larger in size, they are flat, articulating, require power supplies on the wall, and use three different types of wiring. Custom installation is essential. 3) Projector or DLP projector screens are optimally viewed dead on. These are the largest screens available. Their quality can rival that of your local movie theater.

A common mistake made in screen installation is that they are mounted far too high, producing a 30 percent loss of light output. A height of 24-in. from the ground is recommended. Building all equipment into a custom-designed configuration is always optimal.

Complete projection systems have no limitations except for competing light. Thus they are best viewed in a darkened room. Screens are available in sizes ranging from 60-in. up to 200-in. diagonally.

KITCHENS

The personality, needs, and interests of the cook determine the design of an ideal kitchen. Some homeowners are passionate, even semi-professional. Others have full or part-time help. Others still consider the kitchen a laboratory for culinary experimentation. Some enjoy elaborate entertaining, while others prefer simple preparation. Some desire a show place, others a service venue. Cooks who enjoy baking have specific surface and oven requirements. Those who like to grill may want an indoor grill or extra freezer space. A Kosher cook or one who adheres to other religious or health customs will have distinct prescriptions. Even the right-or left-handedness of the cook determines a kitchen's composition.

Once the cook's requirements have been identified, it is helpful to next make a thorough examination of the present kitchen.

Observe:
— Which elements are most appealing?
— Which are insufficient or lacking? (especially counter space and storage)
— Whether the sink and appliances need updating ?
— Whether the room needs additional space for more than one cook, for family gatherings, or for children to do homework?
— Whether it needs to be wired for computerization?

The layout of the new kitchen will also depend on:

Where light enters the room.

What views are most important.

Which walls can be moved or punctured?

Whether the room is big enough for

an island and/or a kitchen table.

When all pragmatic issues have been addressed, the homeowner can surrender to the pleasures of choosing or creating a style. Again, the existing kitchen holds many clues to preferences — conscious and unconscious:

— Is the present style contemporary, transitional, traditional, or Old World? Is this style suitable or would a new and different look be more satisfying?

— Do particular materials or design elements, such as hardwood floors, spindle legs, or arched glass doors, have a strong presence?

— Would the introduction of new materials in backsplashes or counter tops provide a pleasing accent?

— How well does the look of the current hardware work with the kitchen's overall design?

By recognizing these visual or material themes, the homeowner can choose to preserve or radically reinvent the kitchen's look. A similar survey will also reveal preferences for colors and tones. Determine, for example, if the present palette is light, medium, or dark and if that tone will serve the new design.

The personality, needs, and interests of the cook determine the design of an ideal kitchen.

Islands

Islands are wonderfully versatile. They offer preparation, cooking, and serving convenience and are perhaps the easiest way to congregate informally and entertain. The manner in which an island should be equipped will depend on the size of the kitchen and the amount of space left unused by cabinetry and appliances.

Islands are best thought of as a monumental piece of furniture. When well designed they enhance the kitchen with the impact of a great étagère or fine cabinet. Airoom's kitchen designers feel that an island lacking detail will, because of its size and scale, degrade a kitchen. The style of the island should be determined first by the style of the kitchen itself. Is it to be a dramatic architectural statement distinct from that of the room or a harmonious continuation of the overall style? Understand its primary function, and evaluate its size.

Some islands will accommodate sinks, cook tops, a chopping block, even a stove or small refrigerator. Others, more compact, will provide only sufficient space for a service landing, buffet/display, or limited seating. An H-frame, four-legged table island, for example, will not accommodate bookshelves in the way a more traditional structure will.

The minimum width for the walkway surrounding an island is 36-in. Ideally, that width will range between 42-in. and 48-in.

PHOTOS COURTESY OF AIROOM ARCHITECTS & BUILDERS

This island features a prep sink and expansive counter top, greatly enhancing the functionality of the kitchen work space.

Islands can incorporate all kinds of storage based on the homeowners' needs.

An exotic zebra wood and unique design adds an Asian overtone to this kitchen.
Countertop materials feature stone and copper and add an eclectic, upscale feel.

Smooth-surface induction cooktops make for a seamless look.

Island construction can accommodate several large appliances that would otherwise consume precious countertop space. A microwave/convection oven fits nicely into this island.

Appliances

Appliances are continuously evolving in design and technology. From one year to the next, new models are produced that cook faster or more evenly, provide a better way to store refrigerated goods or clean dishes, and have the intelligence to thaw, cook, cool, and reheat food even when the homeowner is not at home.

Today's homeowners need a combination of technology and practicality in the kitchen. To arrive at the proper proportion, it is necessary to understand what proportion of the kitchen is for use, how much is for show, and how much "programming" will actually be used. Some cooks find only gas ranges adequate for proper heat control, for example, while others prefer the world of options that come with copious electronics.

In terms of style, appliances can be hidden away or showcased. Status appliances require pride of place. Those that are to be concealed will need specific architectural or surface treatment.

This design incorporated existing appliances that the client did not want to replace at the time of the remodel.

PHOTOS COURTESY OF AIROOM ARCHITECTS & BUILDERS

"Mixing old and new is an Airoom specialty," says Mike Klein.

Double-ovens are essential in a kitchen used frequently for entertaining. A main course may need to be at roasting temperature, while the simultaneous preparation of a delicate dessert requires a much cooler oven.

Shown on the left, antique furniture can be converted into an elegant piece to house a sink. The use of hand-painted, drop-in tile and wall-mounted faucets completed the look. Note the real French terrazzo floor and use of a salvaged vintage beam.

Cabinetry

All cabinets hold things. Their convenience as well as the quality of their organization and interior and exterior execution are all matters of planning and budget. The quality of a cabinet's construction, surface, and style will depend on the choice of stock production, semi-custom, or fully custom design.

Customization is based on the desired level of detail. Cabinetry can be built into custom widths and depths, for example, with shelves that extend, retract, or have turning lazy susans. Liquor cabinets can be installed with built-in wine coolers and wine storage. Other cabinetry can be designed for display or to hold such items as built-in cappuccino machines, spice racks or rollouts for boxed goods.

More than any other design element, the look and finish of kitchen cabinetry is the primary influence on the room's sensibility.

The detailing of cabinet interiors extends from the shelving installation to the quality of closing mechanisms. Some homeowners want refrigerator drawers in base cabinets, others extra dishwashers. Some choose back and edge lit glass shelves with fiber optic edges, others, metal pull out systems that collapse back into the cabinet with a light touch. Others insist on self-closing doors. Homeowners with children often determine the height of the microwave shelf according to whether they want their kids to be able to use it (lower), or if they wish to shield them (higher). Drawer interiors, too, can be as custom designed as the cabinetry itself — some for precise organization, others for flexibility.

Glass door fronts create a lighter feel in any kitchen. The eye is grounded by the solid feel of the countertops and supporting cabinetry, while the cabinets above create a sense of openness. Colored glass provides additional options.

Counters that slide open for a television to
pop out and swivel, provide possibilities.

Display

In today's kitchens, display is everywhere. Nearly every item, including glass fronted refrigerators, and every surface, including counters that slide open for a television to pop out, provide possibility. Cabinetry and casings that exhibit collections — of everything from spices to porcelains to fancy utensils — must be designed accordingly, i.e. with interior lighting and/or finished interiors. Some homeowners prefer the look of finished wood or a painted interior. Some prefer to accent their collections with glass shelving which can be set inside a display case, hung from the walls or ceiling, and/or lit on any number of sides. A less familiar treatment is the use of opaque or colored glass. Even common food stuffs such as condiments are given prominence: Lidded holders formed flush with the surface of the counter provide ready convenience.

"Soft whites combined with black are classic and timeless," says Klein.

Comfortable circulation around the kitchen table
requires a width of at least 11 or 12-ft.

Shown left, a casual seating area
off the kitchen is perfect for morning coffee.

Kitchen Seating

Comfort is the most practical consideration in
determining the size and location of a kitchen table.
It should be placed so that there is enough distance
between the table and other pieces of furniture or walls
to maneuver around (a minimum of three feet, and
preferably four). The table's access to windows and
other light sources is another important consideration.

Counter seating is always an advantage. Even when
a kitchen has a table, counter seating invites casual
company. Stools, whether backless or not, should fit
easily enough under the counter to easily accommodate
the sitter's leg and knee. Thirty-six inches is standard
height; an ideal counter overhang should be 16-in. or
18-in. wide or more.

Banquettes or window seats offer a picturesque,
informal place for coffee, lounging, and conversation.
They are also practical in kitchens that are tight on
space and where a kitchen table would crowd the room.
Architect Christopher Alexander, in his classic book
"A Pattern Language, writes, "In every room where you
spend any length of time during the day, make at least
one window into a 'window place.'"

PHOTOS COURTESY OF AIROOM ARCHITECTS & BUILDERS

"Always build in the refrigerator when the budget allows. A built-in saves space and gives the kitchen a finished look that a free-standing refrigerator does not." - Mike Klein, Airoom CEO.

An island or workstation may be easily converted
to a desk or additional informal seating.

Matching furniture to the cabinetry creates a
oneness with an informal seating area for two.

A uniform look with stainless
will provide a sleek,
modern atmosphere.

Below, a suspended range hood
adds extra dimension.

BARS & BUTLER'S PANTRIES

Butler's pantries and wine cellars originated in the stately homes and manor houses of Europe. Rooms unto themselves, they accommodated the vast entertaining needs of the royals and gentry. The entertaining needs of today's families and homeowners can be accommodated on a far smaller scale and with far greater convenience. In fact, a bar, butler's pantry or wine cabinet can be designed in almost any room with five feet of available cabinet space.

A one-sided butler's panty, for example, requires approximately six feet in width including two-foot depth for cabinetry. A two-sided butler's pantry will need to be at least eight feet wide. The pantry should have a minimum four-foot walkway.

The size and design of a bar should be based on the style of its use: Will it be a seating area or simply an efficiency bar? Will it be an entertaining spot or a service area? This style of use will also affect the bar's style of design, which should be based on that of the character of the house.

Wine Cellars, Cabinets and Coolers

A modest wine cabinet can be housed in a kitchen closet or in place of built-in shelves. An elaborate butler's pantry can provide space for glass service, cutlery, warming drawers, a sink, and ice makers. Bars and wine coolers can hold as little as wine and liquor or as much as plates, glasses, mixers, coasters, stirs, and condiments.

For serious wine collectors, temperature and humidity controls are crucial. Serious collectors must be concerned, too, with vibrations caused by appliances or other mechanical factors since they can disturb the bottles' delicate sediment.

The ideal temperature of a wine cellar is the same as that of subterranean cellars in France, a consistent 55-60° regardless of the type of wine. The proper relative humidity, 60 percent to 70 percent, keeps corks moist while not inviting mold growth.

PHOTOS COURTESY OF AIROOM ARCHITECTS & BUILDERS

In this wine cellar, Airoom incorporated antique furniture with modern wine storage units. The "old world" feel is reinforced by the frame of loose rock that surrounds the stone floor.

PHOTOS COURTESY OF AIROOM ARCHITECTS & BUILDERS

"For serious wine connoisseurs, it's ideal to have a wine cooler on the main floor, while storage and collectables remain in the basement wine cellar."
- Mike Klein, Airoom CEO

DINING ROOMS

As the interior designer Linda Chase has noted in her book "In Your Own Style," dining room "furniture is meant to serve as a beautiful backdrop that allows the focus of the room to center on the company and the food."

All that is truly necessary to suitably furnish a dining room, regardless of size, is a dining table, serving tables, and comfortable chairs. Attractive wall decorations and lighting are sufficient complements.

"The dining room is the one room of the house that benefits from under furnishing."

- Mike Klein, Airoom CEO

Shape and Size of the Dining Table

The form of the room will dictate the most suitable shape of the dining table. A rectangular or oval table is best for a long room; a circular table is ideal for a square room. A three-foot wide space between the table and service furniture or cabinetry is necessary for the comfortable passage of servers and guests.

The ceiling establishes the height of the room and is thereby a principal element in determining a room's proportions.

Walls and Ceilings

The dining room's innate simplicity compels architectural elements to be beautifully articulated. Wall and ceiling treatments and the use of moldings, panels, and soffits will have especially evident effect. The use of wainscoting, chair rails, picture rails, and crown moldings is a hallmark of traditional style. Their color and application determine the room's formality. A sleek, modern look relies on the finesse of the wall treatment. Their wide range extends from hand painted surfaces, including glazing, washing, lacquering, combing, marbling, and stenciling to murals and wallpapers. Ceilings, except in dining rooms of exceptional height, are best left painted white or a tint of the wall color. A color darker than the color of the walls will diminish the scale and mood of the room.

Room Size

For the comfort of both service and seating, a dining room requires a 12-ft.-by-18-ft. space. 15-by-20-ft. is ideal. A square dining room must be at least 16- or 18-ft. in size. Anything less leaves insufficient room to move chairs in and out or to circulate around service furniture and built-ins.

Lighting

The simplest means of articulating a dining room ceiling is with lighting. If height permits, a chandelier hung over the center of the table is ideal. Wall sconces, which evolved from the metal or glass holder of a candle or glass jet, and cove lighting, which conceals the light source, provide diffused ambient light Low voltage and halogen illuminate decorative displays and tend to create a sense of drama.

BEDROOMS

The bedroom has long since been a place simply for sleep. Today's bedrooms also serve as studies, home offices, gyms, galleries, and entertainment centers. The personality the room is intended to express will determine everything from size and scale to color and furnishing. A softly dressed boudoir makes a sensual setting for retreat and the passions of both body and imagination. A more tailored bedroom will better serve those who wish to retire to a writing desk or reading nook. A modern style bedroom often interests those who prefer to work out and watch TV. Understanding the mood and use of a bedroom is the first step in determining its plan.

— Will the bed have pride of place and how much space will it require?
— What type of closet arrangement is necessary and how many people will be served?
— Is there room for an armoire?
— Is there space for built-in nooks, coves, or window seats?
— Is such furniture as a vanity or reading chair with floor lamp desirable?
— Where will the TV/DVD player best be located?
— If exercise equipment will be kept here, should distinct flooring for it be installed?

"Understanding the mood and use of a bedroom is the first step in determining its plan."
- Mike Klein, Airoom CEO

Bedroom Lighting

The best bedroom lighting is, of course, natural light, and the siting of windows will make all the difference in the quality of the room's mood. A bedroom flooded with sunlight — and especially a view — is always uplifting.

It may require little more than floor and table lamps for adequate illumination. A darker room will benefit from a combination of lighting treatments. Cove and other recessed lighting will maintain a softer ambience. Wall sconces will provide warmth without the harsh exposure of most overhead lights. Reading lamps can be added to bedside tables.

The personality the room is intended to express will determine everything from size and scale to color and furnishing.

The ultimate lighting for the bedroom, of course, is candlelight.

"Taking existing antiques and blending them with modern finishes creates exceptional results." - Mike Klein, Airoom CEO

BATHROOMS

The bathroom is among the most complicated rooms in the house to design. Its function and style must flawlessly cohere in a highly compact space where privacy is paramount.

Even a four-foot square powder room can require the same meticulous planning of space, plumbing, fixtures, flooring, and cabinetry as a master bath. All bathroom plans address, of course, the toilet and sink, and in full baths, the shower and tub. Superior designs also coordinate the following components:

— Switch plates
— Towel bars
— Drain cover
— Shower handle and hinges
— Showerheads and valves
— HVAC registers
— Lighting trim
— Faucet and handles
— Door hardware
— Drawer pulls

Cabinetry and Counters

The style of bathroom cabinetry, more than any other element, determines the style of the room. The choices include everything from the traditional wood vanity, to furniture cut and made into vanities, to the sleekest open leg system with exposed drainage or open racks below. Cabinets can also be installed at the center of the bathroom counter to divide sink areas. Cabinetry fronts on tubs — a sort of wainscoting from the floor up — often include doors that allow easy access to mechanicals for whirlpool tubs. Today's bathrooms tend to have much more upper cabinetry — above the counter. Larger, wider cabinetry, used in place of linen closets, is another popular trend. Open cabinetry allows for rolled up towels and other items to provide color accents.

Bathroom counters today are fabricated from widest imaginable range of materials. The traditional stone, wood, and tile have given way to such modern materials as stainless steel, copper, and zinc. Applications range from inexpensive laminates to complex mosaics in glass, stone, and tile.

Showers and Tubs

In most contemporary bathrooms, the shower takes pride of place over the bathtub. Accordingly, any number of shower amenities is now available, including body sprays with multiple showerheads, handheld showers, "big rain" showerheads, and pull chain showers located over a bench for steam. There are two sided, his-and-hers big showers as large as eight feet in length. Some showers even have places for reclining.

Tubs, on the other hand, have changed little other than in appearance. Some offer therapeutic amenities such as deep steeping, while others have luxury features such as air bubble injection for soaking, relaxation, and meditation. Inline heaters, used especially for whirlpools, keep warm water circulating without constant reheating. Other new trends include chromatherapy and recirculating waterfalls.

Water Conservation

Because the issue of water conservation affects almost every region of the country, systems for restrictive faucets and tank pressurization have become important to many homeowners. One such system — GFX or gravity film exchange — uses a copper coil to surround the drainpipe. As hot water from the shower, washing machine, bathtub, and sinks run down the drainpipe, the GFX's water-filled coils capture the heat and return it to the water heater.

Restrictive faucets, which are mandated in many places, allow for 2 1/2 gallons of water flow per minute. One means for increasing water flow is to install multiple heads and use a larger waterline — a 3/4-in. or 1-in. copper line — directly off the hot water heater. A dedicated water line allows for extra faucets and added water pressure. The installation of pressure tanks in the lower level or basement of a home will provide a hard shower at minimal additional cost.

"The best comfort "bang-for-your buck" are
electric radiant floors" - Mike Klein, Airoom CEO

Floors

In the bathroom, the selection of flooring material revolves not around wear, tear, or practicality, but around style and cost. The most popular choices are stone and tile — hard surfaces that are relatively unaffected by moisture. But with the proper finish, even handsome wood floors are an acceptable choice.

The use of a sealant is imperative in maintaining the floor's condition. With stone, the sealant should be applied both before and after grouting. With ceramic, a grout sealer will preserve the color in the joint and keep it from becoming porous.

Style wise, patterns, inlays, and borders draw color into the bathroom and influence the room's character and feeling of scale.

One of today's greatest bathroom amenities is the heated floor. Electric radiant floors are not a heat source, but an energy efficient comfort system that requires the same amount of energy as a 100-watt bulb. Because they heat only a specified area — around the tub, toilet, and sink — they are inexpensive to operate. The mats through which the radiant heat is conducted come in numerous standard sizes as well as custom configuration. They can be added to a remodeled bathroom floor and are thin enough not to affect the floor's height.

In the bathroom, the selection of flooring material revolves not around wear, tear, or practicality, but around style and cost.

PHOTOS COURTESY OF AIROOM ARCHITECTS & BUILDERS

Contemporary

Toilets

Today's toilets are as simple or as fancy as any homeowner can imagine. From the standard one piece, to the more European style wall hung two piece, to examples within the wall tanks, toilet designs can accommodate any size or style of bathroom. Some come equipped with water jets and blow dryers, other with heated seats, thermostatically controlled. There are those with hydraulic closing seats and others with mechanisms that prevent the seat from banging down. Some even have motors in their tanks to create a bigger siphon jet for flushing.

The minimum distance from toilet centerline to a sidewall is 15-in. The minimum clearance in front of the toilet bowl is 21-in.

Vintage Look

Powder Rooms

Powder rooms afford an important measure of convenience to both guests and family. One as small as 3-by-6-feet can be fitted under a stairway and equipped with a freestanding sink, using a console table. With a wall-hung or corner mounted pedestal sink and a 24-in. doorway, a powder room can fit into a converted closet or be installed in a four-foot square space. A 4-ft.-by-6-ft. rectangle can accommodate one wet wall that contains the plumbing, enabling a powder room of such size and shape to be located off a front hall or back entry. A five-foot square plan with one lopped-off corner is typical of powder rooms located off a main hallway or a stairwell landing.

Lighting

Windows seldom provide sufficient light in bathrooms. Typically they require a combination of general ambient (ceiling or wall sconce) light and specific task lighting over (or on) mirrors. Specialty lighting can be installed on open shelving and in niches and display cases to dress them up and even inside shower stalls. When applying such specialty lighting, certain safety and wear factors must be addressed. For example, steam showers require a housing or canister to deter corrosion.

Mood lighting can be achieved through the use of indirect sources such as floating cabinets, lit underneath.

For a "Grand Hotel" look, the bathroom can be lit with a chandelier.

Bathrooms require a combination of general ambient, as well as specific task lighting.

PHOTOS COURTESY OF AIROOM ARCHITECTS & BUILDERS

Sand-blasted glass is used to create privacy and divide different areas from one and other.

Note the deluxe setup: Rainhead, wall-mounted shower with hand-held sprayer, four strategically placed body sprays, and separate temperature controls.

A dropped ceiling will add extra dimension and emphasis to a space.

A coffer ceiling works with existing architectural style while adding additional visual interest.

A double barrel-vaulted ceiling.

Vaulted open-beam ceiling with exposed structure timbers.

A tin ceiling can capture an old-world feeling.

Crown moldings, intricate medallions and other millwork can set the style and tone of a room.

Vaulted ceiling with wood exposed beam truss, finished in drywall. Additional light is created by the triangular glass on the far plane.

A recessed ceiling creates an extra dimension. Cove lighting emphasizes the space.

French doors can provide transition to either another room or to the outdoors without obstructing a view. For more privacy, the same design can be made of wood panels instead of glass.

Framed glass panels can be used for added drama, particularly when the scale of the home cannot accommodate a double door entry.

Transoms provide additional light, while a simple glass door with basic framing keeps a look more contemporary.

The front door should hold to the architectural style and elements of a home. An extra tall set of doors adds drama, but must be proportional to both the interior and exterior.

An eave emphasizes an entryway and serves to establish a focal point.

Recessed entries establish a shelter from the elements outdoors. A slight curve at the top follows the form of traditional architecture and adds dimension.

PHOTOS AND DETAILS COURTESY OF AIROOM ARCHITECTS & BUILDERS

A good lighting scheme is produced through combinations of daylight and artificial lighting. The type of bulb casting the light will influence the feel of the room as much as its type of delivery. Low voltage incandescent bulbs produce a yellow light that makes a room feel warmer.

Cold-cathode lighting, which emanates from a thin tube, produces very even light in several shades of white as well as colors. These and others can be used in a full array of lighting approaches:

-Cove lighting
-Task
-Display case (cabinet) lighting
-Wall sconces
-Table lamps and floor lamps
-Hanging fixtures
-Outdoor/landscape
-Fiber optics to create effects and mood
-Down lighting
-Recessed
-Low-voltage for artwork, to bring out
 the true color
-Track
-Floor

The use of skylights and cutouts serves as an efficient source of light in a daytime space.

Down lighting via halogen fixtures is cast to highlight cabinets and displays.

Cove lighting is often recessed behind a soffit or ornamental crown molding. If neon is used, color can be incorporated for added drama.

Task lighting serves to properly illuminate a specific area. More often than not, it's used in spaces that require reading.

Grouping fixtures alike in style sets a tone while serving a practical purpose. Sconces add points of interest to guide the eye. Torchere lamps are placed on a console as visual markers. Twin lamps at the base of the stair also coordinate for a complete look.

PHOTOS AND DETAILS COURTESY OF AIROOM ARCHITECTS & BUILDERS

Double pendants can substitute for track lighting if down-lighting is needed.

Lighting a nook with halogen adds drama and emphasis to carved space.

Special consideration should be taken on lighting an exterior, depending on the amount of entertaining taking place outdoors.

Fiber optics add intensity and interest to otherwise ordinary glass shelving.

Recessed lighting encased within the soffit washes the cabinetry.

Correct lighting is critical for capturing the true beauty of artwork.

Interior cabinet lighting creates a soft glow in evening hours.

Hanging a series of fixtures directs light where it's needed most.

A pull-out bin with receptacles for recycling and waste features a cutting station on top.

Cabinet manufacturers have unique cabinet design features to help accommodate extra items.

Here is a clever use of a small space that is left over once the major pieces of cabinetry are in place.

Pull-out shelves allow for easier accessibility to pots, pans and other items below.

Roll-out shelves with built-in containers can create several storage options.

Manufacturers have created special edging on countertops to prevent spills from ever reaching the floor.

Built-in pantries allow for easy accessibility to foods. Taking inventory is a no longer a guessing game when all items are in plain sight. Inset lighting adds an additional aid.

The most important feature is you.

You will need to find a company that will first and foremost, focus around you and your needs. Architects and companies who employ people with large egos may resist input from the client. Such companies may not embrace your rejection of their ideas or your desire for revisions. I found that Airoom Architects and Builders demonstrates just the right mix of professional guidance to help customers unlock the potential of their ideas.

Regardless of whether you are integrating a new space, or revising an existing space, you want to work with a dedicated staff that provides new solutions to old problems while fulfilling your indulgences. Finding a company which knows that you should gain an enhanced lifestyle through your new remodel is the ultimate experience.

Remember that the most important feature in the course of a remodel is you. Employing a firm with the same vision guarantees not only a successful project, but a superior design that you will be proud to call "Home".

For design and build questions, feel free to contact the professionals at Airoom via their web site: www.airoom.com.